A TRUE BOOK®

by
Nancy I. Sanders

Children's Press®
A Division of Scholastic Inc.

New York Toronto London Auckland Sydney
Mexico City New Delhi Hong Kong
Danbury, Connecticut

Children making matzah for Passover

Reading Consultant
Jeanne Clidas, *Ph.D.*
*National Reading Consultant
and Professor of Reading,
SUNY Brockport*

Content Consultant
Rabbi Brant Rosen
*Jewish Reconstructionist
Congregation, Evanston, IL*

Dedication
*For Ben,
who enjoys studying Hebrew*

Library of Congress Cataloging-in-Publication Data

Sanders, Nancy I.
  Passover / by Nancy I. Sanders.- 1st American ed.
    p. cm. — (True book)
Summary: Describes the Jewish holiday of Passover, which
commemorates the exodus of the Jewish slaves out of Egypt.
Includes bibliographical references and index.
  ISBN 0-516-22765-3 (lib. bdg.)   0-516-27779-0 (pbk.)
  1. Passover—Juvenile literature. [1. Passover. 2. Holidays.]
I.Title. II. Series.
  BM695.P3S25 2003
  296.4'37-dc21

                                      2003004533

1 2 3 4 5 6 7 8 9 10 R 12 11 10 09 08 07 06 05 04 03

Contents

Children setting the table for the special Passover meal known as the seder

Looking Back, Looking Ahead

It's spring! For Jewish families, the arrival of spring means it's time to celebrate Passover. This festive Jewish holiday takes place during the **Hebrew** month of Nisan, which falls in March or April depending on the phases of the moon. In Israel, Passover lasts for seven

Passover celebrates how the ancient Israelites escaped to freedom from slavery in Egypt.

days. In countries outside of Israel, Jews celebrate Passover for seven or eight days.

During Passover, Jewish families celebrate the most important event in their history—when they journeyed from slavery in Egypt to freedom. This festival is one of the most important Jewish holidays. Family members both young and old actively participate in age-old traditions. Songs are sung and questions are asked. Stories of freedom are told. Jewish families look forward to a future filled with hope.

Everyone in the family takes part in a Passover seder.

Slaves in a Foreign Land

The Bible tells of how, in ancient times, the **ancestors** of the Jews, or Israelites, settled in Egypt. The Pharaoh, or king, of Egypt made them into slaves. Year after year the Israelites suffered under Pharaoh's cruelty.

The Israelites prayed to God. They cried out and asked God for freedom. In response, God sent them a leader named Moses. Moses went to Pharaoh's court and demanded,

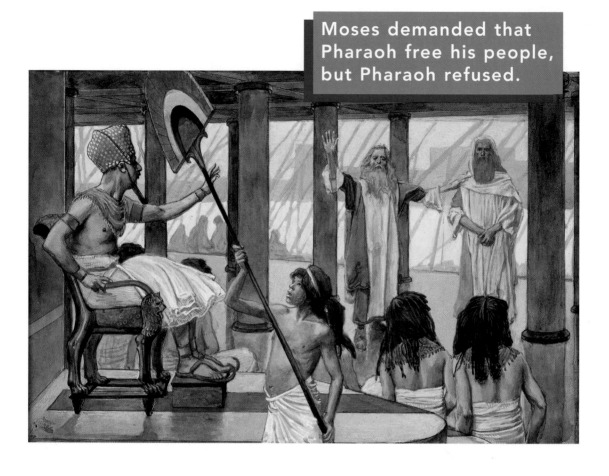

Moses demanded that Pharaoh free his people, but Pharaoh refused.

"Let my people go!" When Pharaoh refused, Moses warned him that God would send punishments to Egypt if the Israelites were not freed. Still Pharaoh refused.

Terrible things started happening to the Egyptians. Their water turned to blood. **Locusts** destroyed their crops. Both the Egyptians and their animals got sick. The sky turned dark in the middle of the day. Nine horrible **plagues**, or troubles, struck the Egyptians.

Frogs and cattle disease were two of the plagues that struck the Egyptians.

The Exodus

Moses warned Pharaoh that if he did not free the slaves, God would send a tenth plague— the worst plague of all. The first-born son in every Egyptian family would die. Pharaoh still didn't listen to Moses.

Moses gave instructions to the Israelites. He said that every Israelite family should

Moses told the Israelites to mark their doorways so that the Angel of Death would pass over their homes.

sacrifice a lamb and serve it as a part of a special meal. They should also mark the doorways of their homes with the blood of this sacrifice.

The mark would let the Angel of Death know to avoid the homes of the Israelites. Moses also told the Israelites to get ready for a journey.

That night, the tenth plague struck. The Angel of Death passed over the Israelites' homes. Only the first-born sons of the Egyptians died. Pharaoh's oldest son was one of those who died.

Pharaoh finally agreed to let the slaves go free. He told

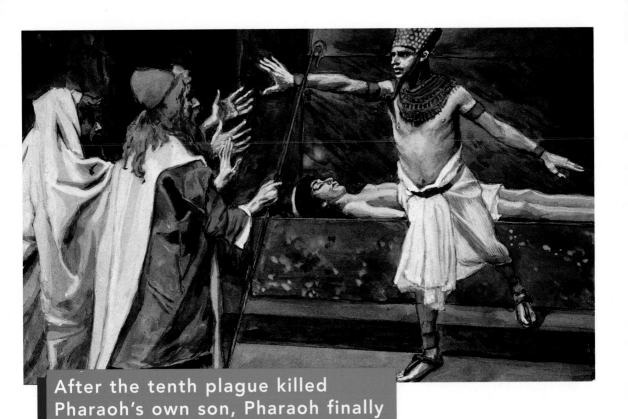

After the tenth plague killed Pharaoh's own son, Pharaoh finally agreed to free the Israelites.

Moses his decision. But Moses knew that Pharaoh might change his mind again, so the Israelites needed to leave as quickly as possible.

This escape from slavery,
which we now call the **Exodus**,
was done with great speed.
There was not enough time for
the Israelites to bake their

bread or even to let it rise. Instead, the Israelites brought their dough along on their journey and baked it under the sun into **unleavened**, or flat, bread called *matzah*.

Matzah, the unleavened bread the Israelites carried and ate during their journey, is the only kind of bread eaten during Passover.

The Israelites left Egypt as quickly as they could. Pharaoh did change his mind, and sent Egyptian soldiers after the Israelites. The Israelites came to the Red Sea and were trapped. God parted the Red Sea and the Israelites crossed over to safety. When Pharaoh's army followed, the water closed in on them and they were drowned.

The name "Passover" comes from the Hebrew word *Pesach* (PAY-sahk), which means "to pass over." During the festival of Passover, Jewish families

remember the night the Angel of
Death "passed over" the houses
of their ancestors. The word
"Passover" has also come to
symbolize the "passing over" of
the Israelites from slavery into
freedom.

The Passover Seder

Jewish families follow age-old traditions during the celebration of Passover. Days before the first night of the holiday, families begin careful preparations. The house is cleaned from top to bottom. A special search for leaven takes place. Leaven is a substance that

A boy helps his mother make a mixture of apples, nuts, and wine called *charoset* in preparation for Passover.

causes bread or dough to rise. Before Passover, *chametz*, food that contains leaven, is completely removed from the house.

A boy hunting for chametz

Many families make a game of searching for chametz. Parents leave small pieces of chametz in each room. The evening before Passover, the family hunts to find them. They carry a candle to help them see. A feather is used to brush up the crumbs into a special spoon. After every bit of chametz is found, it is burned the next morning.

On the first two nights of Passover, the family gathers around the table for a special

The seder table

ceremonial meal called a *seder (SAY-der)*. On the table are dishes and silverware that are used only for Passover. There is also a special seder plate containing symbolic foods, and a plate containing three pieces of matzah covered with a beautiful cloth.

The Seder Plate

Each food on the seder plate has a special meaning.

• The lamb shankbone stands for the sacrificed lamb in the Passover story.

• The roasted egg is a symbol of life, rebirth, and spring.

• Fresh greens also symbolize spring and new life.

• Bitter herbs stand for the bitterness of slavery.

• Charoset—a mixture of apples, nuts, spices, and wine—symbolizes the mortar the Israelite slaves used to construct buildings for the Pharaoh.

A family reading from a Haggadah during a Passover seder

During the seder, the story of Passover is read from a book called a Haggadah and the symbols of Passover are explained. Then the seder meal is eaten.

The word *seder* means "order."
The seder has fifteen steps,
always done in the same order:

Step 1: A **blessing** is said over the
first of four cups of wine or
grape juice. Everyone drinks.

The first blessing
over the wine

Step 2: Hands are washed.
Step 3: Fresh greens
   are dipped in salt water to
   symbolize the slaves' tears.
   A blessing is said, and the
   greens are eaten.

Step 4: The middle matzah is broken into two pieces. The larger piece becomes what is called the *afikoman* and is hidden by the leader of the seder.

A leader of a seder breaking the middle matzah

Traditionally, the youngest person at the seder asks the Four Questions.

Step 5: Children ask the Four Questions about why Passover is celebrated. To answer the questions, Passover stories are told. Everyone drinks the second cup of wine or grape juice.

Step 6: Hands are washed again.

Steps 7 and 8: Two blessings are said over the matzah.

Step 9: Bitter herbs are dipped in charoset and eaten.

Step 10: A sandwich is eaten of matzah, charoset, and bitter herbs.

People eating the sandwich of matzah, charoset, and bitter herbs

Typical foods at a seder meal include matzah-ball soup, *gefilte* fish, chicken, and various kinds of potato or matzah *kugels* (puddings).

Step 11: The meal is enjoyed.

Step 12: Children search for the afikoman. Whoever finds it

gets to demand a prize from the leader of the seder. Everyone eats a bite of the afikoman.

Step 13: A blessing is said after the meal. A blessing is said over the third cup of

Searching for the afikoman

wine or grape juice, and everyone drinks. The door is opened. Everyone hopes that the **prophet** Elijah will visit. A cup of wine has been placed

on the table for him. Stories
of Jewish history are told.
Step 14: Songs are sung to
praise God. A blessing is said
over the fourth cup of wine or
grape juice. Everyone drinks.

At the end of the seder,
everyone sings traditional
Passover songs.

Step 15: The seder ends
with everyone singing lively
traditional songs.

During the week of
Passover, everyone is careful
to eat only food without
leaven. After Passover ends,
holiday dishware is put away
and everyday dishes are
brought back out. Food with
leaven is eaten again.

Freedom and Hope

Jewish people live in countries all over the world. At various times in history, there were countries in which Jews had to hide their beliefs and celebrate Passover in secret. The governments of those countries didn't allow them to practice the Jewish

A family in Israel
celebrating Passover

religion. At times like those, Passover had an even greater meaning. It was a time to dream of freedom for their own families.

Passover is a time for remembering. Jewish people around the world remember the story of the Exodus from Egypt. They remember other important events in Jewish history as well. Families talk about sad times, such as the

During the Holocaust, Jews in many European cities were forced to live in separate neighborhoods called ghettos. Here, residents of the Jewish ghetto of Lodz, Poland, proudly hold up matzah they have baked for Passover.

Holocaust during World War II (1939-1945), when about six million European Jews were killed simply because they were Jewish. Families talk about happy times, too. They remember when Israel, a homeland for the Jewish people, earned its statehood in 1948.

During Passover, older members of the family share their history with younger members. Children are encouraged to ask many questions. These questions and answers help them understand the meaning of Passover.

Everyone is an active participant in the celebration. The prayers, food, symbols, and songs help them remember the past. Passover isn't just about the past, however. It's a holiday when Jews young and old think about the future. Together they share a hope for a future free from **oppression** or hardship for all people.

To Find Out More

Here are some additional resources to help you learn more about Passover:

Books

Hoyt-Goldsmith, Diane. **Celebrating Passover**. Holiday House, 2000.

Musleah, Rahel. **Why on This Night? A Passover Haggadah for Family Celebration**. Simon & Schuster, 2000.

Rose, David and Gill Rose. **Passover** (World of Holidays). Raintree/Steck Vaughn, 1998.

Rush, Barbara. **The Kids' Catalog of Passover: A Worldwide Celebration of Stories, Songs, Customs, Crafts, Food, and Fun**. Jewish Publication Society, 2000.

Segal, Eliezer. **Uncle Eli's Special for Kids Most Fun Ever Under the Table Passover Haggadah**. No Starch Press, 1999.

Organizations and Online Sites

Eileen's Favorite Camp Crafts: Passover Crafts
http://www.chadiscrafts. com/fun/passover.html

This site features a variety of unique Passover crafts you can make.

Fabulous Foods—Passover
http://www.fabulousfoods. com/holidays/passover/pass over.html

From Passover pancakes to brownies, this site has recipes just right for celebrating the holiday.

Passover.net
http://www.chabad-centers. com/passover/

This site is filled with resources. Along with information about Passover and kid-friendly games and activities, you can find a local seder, order matzah, and even ask a rabbi questions.

Passover with Aish
http://www.aish.com/ holidays/passover/family. asp

Find Passover stories, games for the seder, arts and crafts, and Haggadah highlights. This site features appealing artwork and is informative and fun.

Torah Tots: Pesach
http://www.torahtots.com/ holidays/pesach/pesach. htm

There are lots of fun and games on this musical, interactive site. E-mail a Passover card to a friend. Find out all about Pesach and print out pages to color.

Important Words

ancestors relatives who lived long ago

blessing prayer or request for God's favor on someone or something

Exodus departure of the Israelites from Egypt

Hebrew of or having to do with the Jewish people, language, or culture

Holocaust the mass killing of European people, and especially Jews, by the Nazis during World War II

locusts grasshoppers that travel in vast swarms and strip areas of all vegetation

oppression unjust or cruel use of power

plagues troubles that come on suddenly

prophet person who brings a message from God

sacrifice to offer to God

symbolize to stand for; represent

unleavened made without leaven

Index

Meet the Author

When Nancy I. Sanders was a girl, her favorite thing to do was read books. Nancy still loves to read, but now one of the things she enjoys doing is writing. She has authored many books, including craft books, easy readers, nonfiction books, Bible stories, and books for teachers.

Nancy and her husband, Jeff, like to visit places with their sons Dan and Ben. They've toured Yosemite, photographed bison in Yellowstone, and stood on top of the Empire State Building. Nancy and her family live in Chino, California.